The Clever Teens' Guide to

World War Two

Felix Rhodes

Other titles in the series:

The Clever Teens' Guide to

World War Two

Felix Rhodes

Table of Contents

The Road to War

Lasting six years and a day, the Second World War saw the civilian, however young or old, in the frontline of war. Civilian deaths accounted for 5% of those killed during the First World War; but during the Second, of the 50 million plus killed, it was over 66%. During the 2,174 days of the conflict, a thousand people died for each and every hour it lasted. With 81 of the world's nations involved, compared to 28 during the First World War, this war, unlike any other, was total war.

The End of the Great War

The Second World War started on September 1, 1939. But the road to war can be traced back to 1918.

On November 11, 1918, after four long years, World

War One (or the 'Great War' as it was known) came to an end. Germany had been defeated. The victorious nations, mainly Great Britain, France and the USA, met in Paris in 1919. The defeated nations were not invited. Germany was forced to sign a peace treaty, the Treaty of Versailles. Germany had to pay for having started the war and for having caused so much damage. Germans everywhere suffered terrible poverty. The money they had suddenly became worthless. Ordinary Germans greatly resented the treaty and its harsh terms.

From 1919, Germany was ruled by a government voted for by the people but they were unable to control the country. Meeting in the town of Weimar, they established a new constitution, and hence founded the Weimar Republic. But people still blamed the politicians for having lost the war and many began looking for a different political party and a different system. One of these parties was the National Socialists, usually known as the Nazis. Their leader was a man who, like many, had fought in World War One. He blamed Germany's problems on the government and on Germany's Jewish population. His name was Adolf Hitler.

Slowly, over the years, the Nazi Party became more and more popular within Germany. Many Germans believed only Hitler could cure the country's problems.

In January 1933, the German president, Paul von Hindenburg, appointed Hitler his chancellor. (The post of chancellor is similar to the prime minister in the UK).

When, in 1934, Hindenburg died, Hitler took over complete power in Germany. He called himself not the president but the führer, the leader.

Benito Mussolini and Adolf Hitler in Munich, June 1940.

Italy was another country experiencing great change. Italy had been on the Allies' side during the Great War but its people were disappointed by the spoils of victory. The country was crippled by poverty and post-war chaos, not helped by a succession of ineffective governments. People began taking notice of a new, radical voice in Italy – that of

Benito Mussolini, leader of a new party, the Fascists. In October 1922, Mussolini led his followers on a march to Rome and there seized power – first as prime minister, then as dictator. During the 1920s, Hitler admired Mussolini but from 1933, once Hitler was in power, Mussolini found himself increasingly under Hitler's shadow. In 1935, Italy invaded Abyssinia (modern-day Ethiopia), for which Italy was heavily censured by the League of Nations. Isolated from Britain and France, Mussolini found himself drawn into Hitler's orbit. In May 1939, Mussolini signed an alliance with Nazi Germany, the 'Pact of Steel'.

Hitler's ultimate objectives were the destruction of the Jews and the subjugation of lands to the east of Germany. This latter objective was his policy of *Lebensraum*, or extra 'living space' for the German people. He was also determined to extend Germany's influence beyond its borders to areas that had large numbers of Germans. In 1938, Hitler took control of Austria and then, in 1939, Czechoslovakia. Great Britain and France should have stopped him but they allowed Hitler to have his way on the promise that Hitler would not attempt to take over any more countries. Hitler agreed.

Yet, Hitler never took his promises very seriously. In 1939, he began preparations to invade Poland. Britain's prime minister, Neville Chamberlain, promised Poland that if she was attacked, Britain would come to her rescue. France promised the same.

But Hitler wasn't so worried about Britain or France – he was more worried about how the Soviet Union might react. On August 23, 1939, Hitler came to an agreement with the Soviet leader, Joseph Stalin. Poland had Germany as its western neighbour and the Soviet Union as its eastern neighbour, in other words – it was stuck between the two. Stalin agreed not to do anything if Hitler invaded Poland. Indeed, Stalin agreed to attack Poland at the same time.

Days before the invasion, Hitler told his generals to 'close your hearts to pity. Act brutally …The strongest man is right.'

So, on September 1, 1939, Hitler ordered the invasion of Poland.

War Breaks Out

1939

The attack began at 4.45. Attacking from the west, the Germans soon overwhelmed Poland's army. Two days later, on September 3, both Great Britain and France declared war on Germany. But, sadly, in the event, they did nothing. On September 17, the Soviet Union attacked Poland from the east. Poland was crushed.

Hitler's murder of Jews started immediately. Jewish citizens in western Poland, if not already murdered, were herded together into the first ghettos. Nazi Germany made use of Polish workers – over a million being deported to the Reich to work as forced labourers. Proportionately, Poland suffered more than any other country during World War Two – approximately six million, almost one fifth of Poland's pre-war population, perished.

Hitler inspecting troops moving into Poland, September 1939.
German Federal Archives.

The period from the beginning of the war to May 10, 1940, was known in Britain as the 'phoney war', when the war still seemed far away. Children were evacuated to the countryside, rationing was introduced, as was evening time black-outs and the carrying of gas masks.

1940

Meanwhile, Hitler turned his attention to Scandinavia. The supply of iron ore from Sweden to Germany via the northern Norwegian port of Narvick was essential to the

German war machine. Neville Chamberlain sent British ships to protect the port. But first Hitler took over Denmark. Having beaten the Danes within a day, Hitler's army attacked Norway. Germany soon established control of Norway, and put Vidkun Quisling, a Nazi-loving Norwegian, in charge of the country. Hitler trusted Quisling so much that he granted Quisling full license to run the country without interference. Quisling was to remain in charge of Norway until the end of the war. In October 1945, he was executed as a traitor.

Britain's disastrous efforts in Norway brought an end to Neville Chamberlain's time as prime minister. He was replaced, on May 10, 1940, by Winston Churchill. As the new prime minister, Churchill famously declared, 'I have nothing to offer but blood, toil, tears and sweat. We have before us an ordeal of the most grievous kind. We have before us many, many long months of struggle and of suffering. You ask, what is our aim? I can answer in one word: Victory. Victory at all costs'.

On the same day as Churchill became prime minister, Hitler launched his attack on the west. On the May 10, 1940, German forces invaded Luxembourg, Belgium and the Netherlands. Luxembourg surrendered within hours. The Allies, Britain and France, sent their armies but both the Netherlands and Belgium surrendered. The Germans then pushed into France. During the 1930s, the French had built a 280-mile line of fortifications, the Maginot Line. This, they hoped, would prevent a German attack. But the Germans simply attacked north of the line, through the forests of the Ardennes. The Allies expected the Germans to push for Paris, the capital. Instead, the Germans swept north at great speed, pushing the Allies further back until, eventually, they found themselves pinned on the beaches of Dunkirk on the coast of northern France. Hitler's army and air force were poised to destroy them but Hitler ordered them to hold back. Historians have often pondered why Hitler ordered the pause. Perhaps he was still, at this stage, hoping to get Britain onto his side.

With the Allied force poised to be crushed, hundreds of ships, both military and civilian, large and small, set sail from England and between May 26 and June 2 managed to rescue 340,000 Allied troops, a third of whom were French or Belgian.

The defeat at Dunkirk could have been much worse. On June 4, Churchill delivered his much-quoted speech: 'We shall fight on the beaches, we shall fight on the landing grounds, we shall fight in the fields and in the streets, we shall fight in the hills; we shall never surrender'.

Winston Churchill

From the north coast of France, the Germans advanced south.

On June 10, Italy entered the war on the side of its ally, Germany. Mussolini had watched in awe as Hitler's armies marched across Europe, conquering whatever lay in front of him. Determined not to be left behind Italy joined the fight, attacking France in the south.

The French were no match for the Germans. German forces entered a largely deserted Paris on June 14. Two days later, the French appointed 84-year-old Marshal Philippe Pétain prime minister. A hero of the First World

War, Pétain immediately offered to lay down arms.

Hitler in Paris, June 23, 1940. Office of the National Archives.

On June 22, France surrendered. France was to be occupied by the Germans for four long years.

On July 22, under Churchill's orders, Britain formed the Special Operations Executive, the SOE. Its purpose was to coordinate resistance throughout occupied territories or, to use Churchill's phrase, to 'set Europe ablaze'.

Britain Alone

Next, Hitler turned his attention to Britain. Indeed, on June 28, a small part of Great Britain was invaded – the Channel Islands, the only part of Great Britain to be occupied by the Germans throughout the war.

Within ten short months Poland, Denmark, Luxembourg, the Netherlands, Belgium and now France were under Nazi control. Hitler had reached the pinnacle of his rule. The relatively easily-won victories with comparatively modest casualties had won him much admiration in Germany. But his ultimate goal was the Soviet Union. Although plans were already under way, there was still unfinished business in the west; namely Great Britain.

The Battle of Britain and the Blitz

Hitler prepared for the invasion of Great Britain. But before a land invasion could be considered, he had to defeat Britain's Royal Air Force. On July 10, 1940, the Battle of Britain started. Day after day during that summer, German and British fighter pilots fought for dominance in the skies over southern England. The ranks of the RAF were bolstered by large contingents of Canadian and Polish pilots but still they suffered – a quarter of the 1,500 RAF pilots who took to the skies against the *Luftwaffe* were killed in combat.

RAF pilots during the Battle of Britain, 1940.
Imperial War Museum.

On August 20, Winston Churchill praised the brave efforts of Fighter Command in one of his most famous speeches: 'Never in the field of human conflict was so much owed by so many to so few'.

Having failed to defeat the RAF, Hitler changed tact –

on September 7, the first German bombs fell on London. The Blitz had begun. People took to the air raid shelters and often spent nights in London's underground stations. Children were again evacuated to the countryside. Soon, other cities across the UK were targeted – including Glasgow, Belfast, Cardiff, Plymouth, Coventry and many other cities.

The Battle of Britain continued until the end of October. The RAF had held on. Hitler's planned invasion of Britain was to be postponed indefinitely.

From the beginning of the war, Churchill had asked the USA to help. US president, Franklin D Roosevelt, was certainly sympathetic to Britain's call but did not want to commit the US to war in Europe. But the USA did supply the British and other allies with equipment, including ships and planes, oil and food. As a result, the war at sea took on a greater significance. Convoys of merchant ships crossed the Atlantic bringing supplies. Despite being escorted by Britain's Royal Navy and the RAF, the convoys were vulnerable to German U-boats, which, from their bases in occupied France and Norway, hunted in groups or 'wolf packs'. By the end of 1940, more than 4.5 million tons of Allied shipping had been sunk.

On May 9, 1941, a British destroyer attacked a U-boat, and a boarding party managed to capture the German

Navy coding machine and codebooks. Using a huge computer called Colossus, Britain's codebreakers, based in Bletchley Park in Buckinghamshire, were able to decipher German codes. Although they had had some success before, they were now able to do so at will and re-route convoys in order to avoid the wolf packs. Subsequently, within two months, British losses at sea fell by 80 per cent. The cracking of German codes helped the Allies throughout the war in all operations.

The German navy boasted the mighty ship, the *Bismarck*, a sixth of a mile long. On May 24, 1941, on its first mission, the *Bismarck* and accompanying ships fought a fleet of British warships, included the equally-impressive HMS *Hood*, in the Denmark Straits. The battle was intense but brief. The *Hood*, taking a direct hit, was sunk. All but three of its crew of 1,421 men were killed. Britain as a nation was stunned by the loss of the *Hood*. It demanded revenge.

On May 27, the British fleet caught up with the *Bismarck*. Closing in and firing from distances of just two miles, in effect shooting from point blank range, the *Bismarck* was sunk.

Greece and North Africa

Before the war, Mussolini's Italy invaded and ruled over various countries in North Africa – Eritrea, Somaliland and Abyssinia. In September 1940, Mussolini launched another campaign – this time against the British stationed in Egypt. Britain had been *de facto* rulers of Egypt since the 1880s. Egypt was important to Britain because of the Suez Canal which provided British ships the fastest route to Britain's colonial empire in India and the Far East.

Mussolini's African campaign proved disastrous. Far from expanding his empire, Mussolini's possessions in North Africa were dwindling, losing much of his previous conquests. Hitler sent one of his top generals, Erwin Rommel, to aid the beleaguered Italians.

The British and Commonwealth armies and the German and Italian forces fought a see-saw war in North Africa, the Axis pushing the Allies back east into Egypt, then the Allies pushing the Axis back west into Libya. The further one army reached, the further their supply lines were stretched and the easier for the other to fight back.

On October 28, 1940, Mussolini invaded Greece from Italian-occupied Albania. The Greeks, despite only possessing a small army, not only held their ground, but forced the Italians back into Albania. It was another humiliating defeat for the Italian dictator.

Yugoslavia and the Balkans

On April 6, German troops invaded Yugoslavia. On the same day, German forces based in Bulgaria attacked Greece to try and make good Mussolini's disastrous campaign. Progress was rapid. Belgrade, capital of Yugoslavia, was flattened. On April 17, Yugoslavia surrendered.

Greece surrendered on April 23.

Operation Barbarossa

On June 22, 1941, Adolf Hitler launched Operation Barbarossa, Germany's invasion of the Soviet Union. What followed was the most destructive war in history.

Despite signing the agreement with the Soviet Union in August 1939, Hitler had always intended to invade Stalin's empire. Despite the vastness of Russian territory and manpower, Hitler hoped for a quick victory (his generals had predicted ten weeks). In fact, he was so confident of an easy victory in Russia, Hitler only provided his men their summer uniforms, making no provision for the fierce Russian winter that lay further ahead.

Operation Barbarossa was the largest attack ever staged – three and a half million Axis troops, including Italian, Romanian and Hungarian, along a 900-mile front from Finland in the north to the Black Sea in the south. Their tanks were advancing 50 miles a day and, within the first day, one quarter of the Soviet Union's air strength had been destroyed.

German soldiers and a tank advance through Russia, June 1941.
German Federal Archives.

By mid-July, the Nazis had taken Stalin's Baltic States (Lithuania, Estonia and Latvia). Local people helped the roving teams of Nazi death squads to exterminate hundreds of thousands of Jews who were murdered and dumped into huge pits in nearby forests. The most notorious act took place on September 29 – 30 when the Nazis and local collaborators murdered over 33,000 Jews at Babi Yar, outside the city of Kiev in Ukraine.

By the end of August, Axis forces had cut off the Soviet city of Leningrad, subjecting the city to a siege that was to last almost 900 days to January 1944.

More and more Soviet cities fell to the Germans. By the end of October, Moscow was only 65 miles away; over 500,000 square miles of Soviet territory had been captured and huge numbers of Soviet troops and civilians killed or taken prisoner. But with the Russian winter at its most fierce, the Germans were unable to advance and on December 5, had to abandon their plans to attack Moscow.

Pearl Harbor

Japan had also fought in World War One and although they emerged on the winning side, they had little to show for it. Japan viewed its giant neighbour, China, as a means of providing natural resources. Japan's leaders also resented European control of many Asian countries. The only way to rid Asia of its colonial masters, they concluded, was by going to war.

Japan and China had been at war since May 1937. The

US feared Japan, who, in September 1940, had signed an alliance with Germany and Italy. Japan's prime minister, Hideki Tojo, wanted Japan to rule over all of Asia but knew that before that, he had to defeat the US.

On December 7, 1941, six Japanese aircraft carriers positioned themselves 280 miles north of the Hawaiian island of Oahu. At 07.50, Japanese planes attacked the US fleet anchored at the port of Pearl Harbor. By 10 a.m. it was all over – three of the eight American battleships had been sunk and four seriously damaged; many other vessels were destroyed together with almost 300 planes. 2,403 Americans died (civilian and military) and over 1,000 wounded. The Japanese lost 29 planes and 100 pilots.

December 7, according to President Roosevelt, was a 'day of infamy'. As a result, the US declared war on Japan. Churchill was delighted. Adolf Hitler too was pleased: On December 11, Germany (and Italy) declared war on the US. The war, that had started 27 months before, was now truly global.

The USS West Virginia in flames, Pearl Harbor,
December 7, 1941.

The Philippines and Burma

At the same time as Pearl Harbor, Japanese forces attacked the Philippines (a US territory since 1898). American and Filipino forces were forced to flee from the Philippines capital Manila to the Bataan peninsula, then onto the island of Corregidor.

With no reinforcements available and with the Americans suffering from hunger, malaria and low morale, the Japanese caught up and on April 9, forced the 70,000 remaining American and Filipinos on Corregidor onto a seven-day, 65-mile 'Death March' into captivity. One sixth

21

died on route – shot or bayoneted by their captors. Only a third survived to liberation 3½ years later.

Within hours of the attack on Pearl Harbor, Japanese forces attacked and subsequently occupied the British colony of Hong Kong, British-controlled Malaya, neutral Thailand and various US Pacific islands. Hong Kong surrendered on Christmas Day, 1941 – 'Black Christmas'. On December 21, Thailand and Japan signed an alliance. A month later, Thailand declared war on the US and Britain.

On December 11, 1941, the Japanese landed on the southern tip of the British colony, Burma. They were determined to block Burmese supplies reaching China on the 700-mile long 'Burma Road'. The Japanese proceeded north, forcing the British to retreat 1,000 miles into India, the longest retreat in British military history.

The people of India and Australia feared they'd be next.

The Fall of Singapore

Amongst its many colonial possessions, Great Britain ruled over the nation of Malaya. The island of Singapore, 273 square miles, on the southern tip of Malaya was considered a prize asset. It was meant to be an impregnable fortress. But on December 7, at the same time as their comrades were launching their attack on Pearl Harbor, the Japanese landed on Malaya on the north-eastern coast, 620 miles to the north of Singapore. Slowly but surely, the Japanese inched southwards. On February 15, 1942, Japanese troops forced the surrender of Singapore, a defeat often considered Britain's worst humiliation in its military history. Over 80,000 British, Australian and Indian troops were to spend the rest of the war in captivity. Half of them would never return home.

Wannsee

During 1941, the Nazis had come to the conclusion that the killing of Jews on the edges of pits was too time-consuming. Instead, they began experimenting with gas. This, they decided, provided a more rapid and 'efficient' means of murder. On January 20, 1942, fifteen top Nazis (but not Hitler) met in a grand villa on the banks of Berlin's Lake Wannsee. The meeting discussed escalating the killing to a new, industrial level, what they referred to as the 'Final Solution of the Jewish Question'.

On February 15, 1942, the first transport of Jews from Upper Silesia arrived in Auschwitz, all of them gassed on arrival. The Nazis established six main death camps in occupied Poland specifically designed for killing:

23

Auschwitz-Birkenau, Belzec, Chelmno, Majdanek, Sobibor and Treblinka.

The Pacific War

The US had managed to break Japan's naval codes. As a result, on May 4, 1942, an American fleet intercepted a Japanese fleet on the Pacific Ocean on its way to New Guinea. The Battle of the Coral Sea was a battle of aircraft carriers, fought with planes, the first sea battle where the opposing fleets never came within sight of each other. Neither side emerged as the clear victor. A second sea battle, a month later, the Battle of Midway, resulted in a decisive American victory, and, as well as diminishing the strength of the Japanese navy for the rest of the war, allowed the US to begin its counter-offensive.

The Americans bombed the islands of New Guinea while the US Navy inflicted an effective blockade, resulting in mass starvation for both the Japanese defenders and the island inhabitants, forcing the Japanese into cannibalism.

On April 18, 1942, sixteen US bombers took off from an aircraft carrier 800 miles from Japan and bombed Tokyo, inflicting the first bombing raid, albeit on a small scale, against Japan.

In May 1942, the Japanese invaded and occupied the

Solomon Islands. Given its proximity to New Zealand and Australia's northern coast, the islands became an important objective for both the Japanese and the Allies. On August 7, 1942, 10,000 American troops landed on the island of Guadalcanal, the first American ground offensive of the war. It proved to be bloody and brutal confrontation. Eventually in February 1943, the longest battle of the Pacific war, the remaining Japanese evacuated. Guadalcanal was the first objective in what the Americans called 'island hopping', taking one island at a time before launching a full-scale attack on Japan itself.

A wounded American soldier during the Guadalcanal campaign, February 1943.

The Japanese war on China continued. The Japanese objective was simple and brutal: the "Three Alls: kill all, loot all; burn all". The Japanese set up a number of facilities in order to experiment on human guinea pigs. The most notorious was 'Unit 731' in the city of Harbin in north-east China. Here, tens of thousands of Chinese civilians, including the elderly and infants and pregnant women, died as a result of experiments conducted without anaesthesia, including being injected with diseases and subjected to weapon testing, such as human targets for the testing of flamethrowers. (Unfortunately, after the war, the US granted the leading practitioners of Unit 731 immunity from punishment on condition they passed all their findings to the Americans.)

Prisoners of war suffered terribly. To surrender was, for the Japanese, a dishonourable act, even for the last man, and those that had surrendered were not worthy of dignity or life. As a result, one in four Allied prisoners of war (POWs) died in Japanese camps compared to one in twenty held prisoner by the Germans. Between November 1942 and October 1943, 60,000 POWs were used alongside some 200,000 civilians to construct the infamous Burma Railway, a 250-mile stretch of rail track and bridges through dense jungle, linking Burma to Thailand. Working in appalling conditions, severely malnourished and beaten, almost half the civilian workforce died, and up to 14,000 POWs.

Stalingrad

The citizens of Leningrad fought for survival as the Germans besieged the starving city. Limited supplies of food were brought in from the east over Lake Ladoga – by boat during summer and by lorry over the frozen waters during winter – but there was never enough and cannibalism was rife.

On June 28, 1942, Hitler launched Operation Blue in order to capture the vital Russian oil fields in the Caucasus and the city Stalingrad on the River Volga. Led by the Sixth Army, Germany's largest wartime army, commanded by General Friedrich Paulus, the Germans were fully expecting a total victory as they pushed the Soviet forces back. By August 23, the German advance had reached the outskirts of Stalingrad and, with 600 planes, unleashed a devastating aerial bombardment. Entering the city, the Germans, along with their Axis comrades, comprising of Italians, Romanians and Hungarians, fought the Soviets street for street, house for house, sometimes room for room.

Stalin charged Georgi Zhukov to defend the city and

formulate a plan to repulse the invader. On November 19, 1942, the Soviet Red Army launched Zhukov's carefully-planned counteroffensive. Within four days, the Soviet attack had totally encircled the beleaguered German forces.

The Soviets squeezed the 250,000 Germans and their Axis comrades tighter and tighter. As the feared Russian winter set in and temperatures dropped to the minus forties, starvation, frostbite, disease and suicide decimated the Germans. Medical facilities were, at best, crude.

Captured German soldier, Stalingrad, January 1943.
German Federal Archives.

On January 24, 1943, Paulus requested permission to surrender. Hitler refused, saying it was the Sixth Army's historic duty to stand firm to the 'last man'.

On the 30th, the tenth anniversary of his coming to power, Hitler promoted Paulus to the rank of field marshal on account that no German field marshal had ever surrendered. The following day, however, Paulus did.

Hitler, 1,000 miles away, was livid.

Two days after Paulus' surrender, on February 2, 1943, the remnants of his stricken army also surrendered; the Battle of Stalingrad was lost.

Stalingrad marked the beginning of the end for the Axis on the Eastern Front. Slowly but inexorably, the Soviets fought back.

The Beginning of the End

North Africa and Kursk

The Allies and Axis were still fighting across the reach of North Africa. In October 1942, the Axis went on the offensive, attacking the British in the small town of El Alamein in Egypt. The British held their ground and under the stewardship of Bernard Montgomery won a famous victory, ending the Axis threat to Egypt and the Suez Canal. Winston Churchill was delighted, saying: "this is not the end. It is not even the beginning of the end. But it is, perhaps, the end of the beginning."

Australian troops during the Second Battle of El Alamein, October 1942. Imperial War Museum.

On November 8, 1942, an Anglo-American force landed in Morocco. Within three days, the Allies had control of over a thousand miles of the north-western African coast. Finally, on May 8, 1943, the Axis surrendered unconditionally to the Allies. Hitler's African adventure was at an end.

But on the Eastern front, Hitler wasn't quite finished yet. The industrial city of Kursk, 320 miles south of Moscow, had been captured by the Germans in November 1941, and retaken by the Soviets in February 1943. Hitler was determined to recapture it.

The climax of the Battle of Kursk took place near a village called Prokhorovka on July 12, when one thousand tanks and a thousand aircraft on each side clashed on a two-mile front, fighting each other to a standstill. After a month of intense fighting, the Germans ran out of energy and resources.

Losses on both sides were huge but with the Soviet Union's vast resource of manpower and with huge amounts of aid coming in from the US, Stalin could sustain his losses. Hitler, however, could not. Germany never again launched an offensive in the East.

In January 1944, after almost 900 days, the epic and devastating Siege of Leningrad was lifted. Over one million civilians had died in Leningrad from German bombs and artillery, from disease, the cold or starvation.

Italy

The Allies, now with the Americans firmly in charge, launched their campaign against Mussolini's Italy. On July 10, 1943, they landed on the island of Sicily, on the southern tip of Italy, where they enjoyed an ecstatic welcome from the islanders. Mussolini appealed to Hitler to send reinforcements but with German forces tied up on the Eastern Front, no help was forthcoming.

As a result of the invasion of Sicily and the critical situation now facing Italy, Mussolini was disposed. Mussolini was arrested and imprisoned. The Italian population, who once supported Mussolini, rejoiced.

On September 3, 1943, the same day that Allied troops landed on mainland Italy, Italy signed an armistice and, five days later, swapped sides and joined the Allies. On October 13, Italy declared war on Germany, its former ally.

Meanwhile, Mussolini was imprisoned in a hotel high up on the mountains of Gran Sasso in central Italy. It was here, on September 12, that Mussolini was dramatically rescued by a crack team of German commandoes. On Hitler's orders, Mussolini was returned to German-occupied northern Italy as the puppet head of a fascist republic based in the town of Salo on Lake Garda. But Mussolini's power was limited and any decision had to be agreed by Berlin.

The Allies' advance up the Italian peninsula was slow and difficult. But, bit-by-bit, they pushed the Germans back, beginning with the capture of Naples on October 1, 1943. Having overcome a determined stand at the epic Battle of Monte Cassino between January and May 1944, the Allies advanced on German-held Rome, which they took on June 4.

D-Day

With Italy almost secured and with the Soviet Union's Red Army advancing from the east, it was time to launch the much-anticipated invasion of northern Europe. Two years earlier, in the early hours of August 19, 1942, the Allies had attacked the port of Dieppe on France's northern coast, 65 miles across from England. The operation proved a disaster. The German defenders at Dieppe easily fought off the attack, killing 1,027 Allied troops.

Despite the failure of Dieppe and the high rate of losses, important lessons were learned – that a direct assault on a well-defended harbour was not an option for any future attack; and that superiority of the air was a prerequisite. Hitler too felt as if a lesson had been learned. Knowing that at some point the Allies would try again, he ordered the building of the 'Atlantic Wall'. Employing two million labourers from across Nazi-controlled Europe, many of them slave workers, construction began on a line of fortifications that, once completed, spread 2,800 miles along the coast of the whole of Western Europe – from the northern tip of Norway, along the coasts of Denmark, Germany, the Netherlands and Belgium, along France's Channel and Atlantic coasts and down to the border of neutral Spain in the south.

In planning the invasion of Nazi-occupied France, the Allies went to great lengths in deceiving the Germans as to when and where the anticipated invasion might take place. The various ruses worked so on June 6, the five Normandy beaches were not as heavily defended as might have been.

June 6, 1944, D-Day. Gliders and parachutists landed behind the German lines capturing the first bit of occupied territory – Pegasus Bridge. At 05.50, 138 Allied ships, positioned between three and thirteen miles out, began their tremendous bombardment of the German coastal defences. Above them, one thousand RAF bombers attacked, followed in turn by one thousand planes of the USAAF. 150,000 soldiers landed on the beaches. They were fiercely resisted, especially on one of the US-designated beaches, Omaha.

Hitler urged a swift counterattack, but with insufficient troops and air power, Rommel's men fell back and slowly, over the coming days and weeks, the Allies edged forward.

By June 27, US troops had taken the vital port of Cherbourg as the Allies began their advance southwards. On August 15, a second invasion on France began in the south. On August 23, Paris was liberated.

German prisoners of war, June 6, 1944. Imperial War Museum.

The Approach from the West

The Allies began their thrust eastward, liberating Brussels and Antwerp on September 3 and 4 respectively. On the September 10, US troops liberated Luxembourg. On the same day, at the German-Dutch-Belgium border town of Aachen, Allied troops set foot on German soil for the first time since the beginning of the war. But it took until October 21 until Aachen was secured.

But the German war machine wasn't finished yet. Hitler's scientists had long been working on a series of 'wonder weapons' that, Hitler hoped, would turn the tide of war back in his favour. On the June 13, 1944 Germany launched one of these new, terrifying weapons against Great Britain – the V1 rocket, or flying bomb. Flying at about 350 miles per hour, the first attack hit London's East End, killing eight. Within three weeks, 2,500 Londoners had been killed by the V1. Then, three months later, came the even more terrifying V2s, which, unlike the V1, could not be seen or heard as a V2 travelled faster than the speed of sound. Anti-aircraft guns, which could intercept a V1, were useless against the V2.

But, although effective, the V1 and V2s came too late to alter the course of the war.

On July 20, 1944, a group of German officers, hoping to make peace with the Allies and save Germany from further destruction, tried to assassinate Hitler at his 'Wolf's Lair' headquarters in East Prussian. The plot failed and anyone involved with the plot, however remotely, was rounded-up, imprisoned, tortured or executed.

On December 16, 1944, Hitler launched a last-ditch counter-offensive through the Ardennes forest in Belgium. Despite some initial success in what became known as the Battle of the Bulge, the Germans soon lost the impetus and the Allies, having suffered grievous losses, surged forward again. By the end of January 1945, the line was back to where it was on December 16. But at a cost – the US lost over 80,000 men killed or wounded. The Germans had lost over 100,000 and, vitally, much of its aircraft and tanks which, at this stage of the war, were impossible to replace. The march on Berlin was back on.

US troops slogging through Belgium during the Battle of the Bulge, January 1945.

While the ground troops slogged through France, the Low Countries and into Germany itself, the RAF and its

American equivalent were bombing Germany. Many German cities were targeted but it is the bombing of Dresden in Eastern Germany, and its utter destruction, that caused the greatest shock.

2,640 tons of bombs were dropped on Dresden. A firestorm erupted in an area eight miles square reaching temperatures of 1,500 degrees centigrade engulfing the narrow, medieval streets. Dresden had been obliterated. The Germans had began the war bombing UK cities – now it was their turn to suffer: "They sowed the wind; and now they are going to reap the wind," as said by the man in charge of Britain's Bomber Command during the latter part of the war, Sir Arthur Harris.

The Approach from the East

From the summer of 1944, with the Soviet army advancing steadily on the Third Reich, it became apparent to the Nazis that they had to retreat. In doing so, they tried to destroy the evidence of what had taken place in the extermination camps of Poland.

Hundreds of thousands of people were still alive in the Polish camps who would be able to testify against the Nazis if they survived. Operations therefore began to evacuate the surviving Jews, Soviets, Poles, Communists,

Jehovah's Witnesses, homosexuals and other prisoners towards concentration camps in Germany. They were marched westwards into the Reich for weeks on end. Anyone unable to keep up was shot and left by the roadside.

The first camp to be liberated by the Soviets, on July 23, 1944, was Majdanek, on the outskirts of the city of Lublin. Other camps soon followed – Belzec, Sobibor and Treblinka amongst others.

By the end of 1944, the Red Army had driven the Germans out of Ukraine, Belorussia (now called Belarus), Hungary, Romania, Bulgaria, Latvia, Lithuania, Estonia and Poland. It was, for the Russians, the "Year of the Ten Victories".

On January 27, 1945, the Soviets liberated Auschwitz, where they found around 7,600 starving prisoners who had been too weak to leave and had thus been left behind to die.

Bergen-Belsen in Germany was the only camp liberated by the British. Tens of thousands had died of disease and starvation. One of its victims was Anne Frank who, along with most of her family, perished there in March 1945. After the liberation on April 15, 1945, mass graves were dug to hold 5,000 bodies *each* and contemporary film footage shows corpses being bulldozed into these pits.

Such images shocked the world.

Liberation of prisoners at Auschwitz, January 1945.

For those living in East Prussia, the approaching Soviet army was frightening. Hundreds of thousands of German civilians fled west, hoping to escape the Russians close behind.

In Eastern Europe, Poland once again became a focal point. On August 1, 1944, with the Soviets bearing down on Poland, the Polish Underground Army in Warsaw staged an uprising. It began well for the Poles. But soon, the battle-hardened Germans fought back. Soviet forces, a mere twelve miles away, could have helped the Poles. But Stalin, more than happy to see the Polish Home Army destroyed, refused. In addition, Stalin refused to allow his western Allies use of Soviet air bases to airlift supplies to the struggling Poles. Without Allied support, the Poles' brave stand was doomed and the uprising came to an end on October 2.

Endgame

1945

On April 12, 1945, US president, Franklin Roosevelt, died aged 63, to be replaced by Harry S Truman. The news of Roosevelt's death brought joy to the German high command, but their joy was short-lived. On April 23, Soviet forces entered Berlin. Two days later, Soviet troops met their American counterparts in the town of Torgau on the River Elbe.

Meanwhile, on April 27, in northern Italy, the former Italian dictator, Benito Mussolini, tried to escape to the safety of Switzerland. But he was caught by communist Italians. The following day, April 28, Mussolini was shot. His body, along with a few others, was dumped in the back of a truck and driven back to Milan and delivered to the main square where they were left to hang upside down, for public display, from a rusty beam outside a petrol station.

In January 1945, with the Soviet Red Army bearing down on Germany, Hitler had left his HQ in East Prussia and moved back to Berlin and into the Reich Chancellery. A month later, he went underground into the Chancellery's air-raid shelter, a cavern of dimly-lit rooms made of solid, high-quality concrete.

Hitler refused to leave Berlin, and finally, realizing the war was truly lost, he decided to end his life. On April 20, Hitler celebrated (of sorts) his 56th birthday. A week later, just past midnight on April 29, in a ten-minute ceremony, Hitler married his long-term partner, Eva Braun.

On April 30, Hitler and his wife of forty hours committed suicide, Hitler by shooting himself in the temple. The bodies were carried out into the Chancellery garden and set alight.

On May 2, Berlin surrendered. On May 7, Germany surrendered.

The war in Europe had come to an end.

Soviet soldiers hosting the Soviet flag following the Battle of Berlin, May 1945. German Federal Archives.

Liberation of the Far East

In August 1944, the Pacific island of Guam was finally retaken. It had been occupied by the Japanese since December 8, 1941, the day after Pearl Harbor. Some ten per cent of Guam's pre-war population had been killed during the 31 months of Japanese occupation.

On October 20, 1944, US and Filipino troops landed on the eastern side of the island of Leyte, beginning the liberation of the Philippines.

On February 19, 1945, US marines landed on the small Pacific island of Iwo Jima, part of the Bonin Islands. Only eight miles square and less than 700 miles from Tokyo, it was, for the Japanese, vital to save it from becoming a base for the enemy. Thus, there were 20,000 Japanese troops based on this small island. The battle was, as always, ruthless. It took until March 26 before the Americans prevailed, during which time 30,000 of them had been killed.

The US's bombing campaign against Japan did not start in earnest until late 1944. The B-29 planes were capable of attacking from such high altitude that they were beyond the reach of Japan's anti-aircraft guns. Raids intensified from early spring 1945. But it was the raid on the night of March 9–10, 1945 that was the most devastating. Estimates vary but at least 80,000 people and possibly up to 150,000 were killed in this one raid alone, dwarfing even Dresden a month earlier. It remains the most destructive bombing raid in history.

On April 1, American troops had landed on the large island of Okinawa (460 square miles), 340 miles from mainland Japan. It took 13 weeks of intense, brutal fighting to defeat the 100,000-strong Japanese defenders. Finally, on June 22, Okinawa was theirs.

With Okinawa in American hands, mainland Japan was within touching distance. But the intensity of the Pacific campaign made the US think twice about launching a ground invasion of Japan. Plans were certainly in preparation but US planners feared a very high rate of Allied and civilian casualties, numbering in the millions. Thoughts turned instead to an alternative.

Hiroshima and Nagasaki

Japan was as good as defeated but when presented with the opportunity to surrender Japan refused.

Faced with a long war in the Far East, President Truman took decisive action – at 8.15 on the morning of August 6, 1945, the American plane, the *Enola Gay*, dropped an 8,000-pound atomic bomb on the city of Hiroshima, 500 miles from Tokyo. The effects were devastating. Every building within a 2,000-yard radius of its centre was vaporized. Some 140,000 were killed immediately.

But still the Japanese refused to surrender. So, three days after Hiroshima, the Americans dropped a second atomic bomb on Nagasaki.

On the same day as Nagasaki, the Soviet Union attacked the Japanese in occupied Manchuria, ahead of invading Japan itself.

The Japanese had a number of frantic talks over whether to surrender or not. In the end, they decided, in the face of these 'new, most cruel bombs', as the Japanese emperor called them, they had no choice. And so on August 15, Japan surrendered.

The destruction of Hiroshima, August 6, 1945.

The formal surrender took place in Tokyo Bay on board an American battleship on September 2, 1945 – six years and a day after Germany's invasion of Poland. A week later, on September 9, Japan formally surrendered to China.

The Second World War was truly over. Now came the torturous years of peace.

World War Two Timeline

1939

September 1 Germany invades Poland.

September 3 Britain and France declare war on Germany.

September 17 Soviet Union invades eastern Poland.

September 27 Surrender of Warsaw.

1940

April 9 Germany invades Denmark and Norway.

May 10 Germany invades Belgium, Holland and Luxembourg.

May 10	Winston Churchill becomes British Prime Minister.
May 13	Bombing of Rotterdam.
May 15	Holland surrenders to Germany.
May 26	Start of the Dunkirk evacuation.
May 27	Belgium surrenders to Germany.
June 10	Capitulation of Norway.
June 10	Italy declares war on Britain and France.
June 14	Germans occupy Paris.
June 18	Soviets annex Baltic States.
June 22	France signs armistice with Germany.
June 30	Germany begins occupation of the Channel Islands.
July 10	Battle of Britain begins.
July 11	Petain becomes head of French Vichy Government.
September 13	Italy invades Egypt.
September 15	Climax of Battle of Britain.
September 27	Germany, Italy and Japan sign Tripartite Pact.
October 28	Italy invades Greece.
November 14	Greek army repels Italians back into Albania.
November 22	Italian army defeated by Greeks.
December 9	British offensive begins in North Africa.

1941

March 30	German Afrika Korps begins offensive in North Africa.
April 6	Germany invades Yugoslavia and Greece.
April 12	Germans occupy Belgrade.
April 27	Germans capture Athens.
May 24	The HMS *Hood* is sunk
May 27	The *Bismarck* is sunk.
June 22	Operation Barbarossa - Germany invades Soviet Union.
June 22	Italy and Romania declare war on Soviet Union.
September 15	Siege of Leningrad starts.
December 5	Germans abandon attack on Moscow.
December 7	Japanese attack on Pearl Harbor.
December 7	Japan invades Malaya.
December 8	USA and Allies declare war on Japan.
December 11	Germany and Italy declares war on USA.
December 11	Japan attacks Burma.
December 25	Japanese capture Hong Kong.

1942

January 2   Japanese capture Manila.

January 21   Japan invades Burma.

February 15   Singapore falls to the Japanese.

April 30   Japanese close Burma Road.

May 6   Fall of Corregidor and surrender of US forces on the Philippines.

May 4-8   Battle of Coral Sea.

May 27   Japanese complete conquest of Burma.

June 4   Battle of the Midway.

August 7   US forces lands on Guadalcanal.

August 19   Britain's Dieppe Raid.

August 22   Germany's Stalingrad offensive begins.

October 23   Second Battle of El Alamein begins.

November 8   Allies invade French North Africa.

1943

February 2   German surrender at Stalingrad.

May 13   Axis forces in North Africa surrender.

July 4   Battle of Kursk begins.

July 10   Allies land in Sicily.

July 25   Overthrow and imprisonment of Mussolini.

August 18   Allied conquest of Sicily complete.

September 2 Italy signs armistice.

September 3 Allies land in southern Italy.

September 8 Italy surrenders. Germans occupy Rome.

September 12 Mussolini rescued.

September 23 Mussolini declares Fascist government in Northern Italy.

October 1 Allies capture Naples.

October 13 Italy declares war on Germany.

1944

January 27 End of Leningrad siege.

February 15 Allies destroy monastery of Monte Cassino.

June 4 Allies enter Rome.

June 6 Operation Overlord – Allied invasion of Normandy.

June 13 German 'V-1' offensive begins against Britain.

June 27 US forces captures Cherbourg.

July 20 Attempted German assassination of Hitler.

August 1 Polish uprising in Warsaw.

August 15 Allies invade southern France.

August 25 Allies liberate Paris.

September 3 Allies liberate Brussels.

September 4 Allies liberate Antwerp.

September 8	German 'V-2' offensive begins against Britain.
October 2	End of Warsaw Uprising.
October 4	Allies land in Greece.
October 14	Allies liberate Athens.
October 19	US invades Philippines.
October 20	Liberation of Belgrade.
Oct 21-22	Battle of Leyte Gulf.
October 23	Soviets enter East Prussia.
November 4	Surrender of Axis forces in Greece.
December 16	German attack through Ardennes - Battle of the Bulge begins.

1945

January 1	Germans withdraw from Ardennes.
January 17	Soviets liberate Warsaw.
January 26	Soviets liberate Auschwitz.
January 27	'Burma Road' re-opened.
February 13	Allies bomb Dresden.
February 19	US invades Iwo Jima.
March 7	US cross the Rhine.
March 17	US capture Iwo Jima.
April 1	US invades Okinawa.
April 12	US President Roosevelt dies, replaced by

Harry S Truman.

April 23 Soviets enter Berlin.

April 25 Soviet and US forces meet at the River Elbe.

April 28 Mussolini captured by partisans and executed.

April 30 Hitler commits suicide.

May 2 German forces in Italy surrender.

May 4 German forces in Holland, Denmark and North-West Germany surrender.

May 7 German unconditional surrender to the West.

May 8 German unconditional surrender to the East.

May 9 Liberation of Channel Islands.

June 22 US forces capture Okinawa.

August 6 Atomic bomb dropped on Hiroshima.

August 8 Soviet Union declares war on Japan.

August 9 Atomic bomb dropped on Nagasaki.

August 14 Japan agrees to surrender.

September 2 Formal Japanese surrender.

Images

All the images used in this book are, as far as the publisher can ascertain, in the public domain. If they have mistakenly used an image that is not in the public domain, please let them know at felix@historyinanhour.com and they shall remove / replace the offending item.